# SCENE BY SCENE COMPARATIVE WORKBOOK HL17

# The Plough and the Stars

by Seán O'Casey

Theme/Issue - Relationships

Literary Genre

General Vision and Viewpoint

Copyright © 2016 by Amy Farrell.

All rights reserved. No part of this publication may be reproduced, distributed or transmitted in any form or by any means, including photocopying, recording, or other electronic or mechanical methods, without the prior written permission of the publisher, except in the case of brief quotations embodied in critical reviews and certain other noncommercial uses permitted by copyright law. For permission requests, write to the publisher, addressed "Attention: Permissions Coordinator," at the address below.

Scene by Scene
11 Millfield, Enniskerry
Wicklow, Ireland.
www.scenebysceneguides.com

info@scenebysceneguides.com

The Plough and the Stars Comparative Workbook HL17 by Amy Farrell. —1st ed.
ISBN 978-1-910949-39-9

# The Plough and the Stars Comparative Study Workbook

This workbook is designed to help Leaving Certificate English students become familiar with the Comparative Study modes and to understand how each mode may be applied to *The Plough and the Stars*.

The Comparative Study Modes at Higher Level for 2017 are:

### Theme/Issue

The theme covered in this workbook is Relationships. This theme can be applied to any relationship in a text and covers love, marriage, friendship and family bonds.

Consider the complexities of relationships and the impact they have on characters' lives.

### Literary Genre

This mode refers to the way the story is told.

Consider aspects of narration such as the manner and style of narration, characterisation, setting, tension, literary techniques, etc.

### The General Vision and Viewpoint

This mode refers to the author's outlook or view of life and how this viewpoint is represented in the text.

Consider whether the text is bright or dark, optimistic or pessimistic, uplifting or bleak, etc.

## How Does it Work?

This workbook has three parts, one each for Theme/Issue (our chosen theme for study is Relationships), Literary Genre and General Vision and Viewpoint. Each part has three sections: Know the Text, Know the Mode and Compare the Texts.

### Know The Text

These questions are on *The Plough and the Stars* text and refer specifically to this play. Through answering these questions you will get to know the text well, while also getting a feel for the Comparative Study mode the questions relate to.

### Know the Mode

These questions use 'mode' specific terms and phrases and are intended to help prepare you for tackling exam questions. They focus on the mode itself, rather than the text you have studied. You apply your knowledge of the text to the mode in question.

### Compare the Texts

These questions ask you to compare your texts under specific aspects of each mode. It is important that you get used to the idea of comparing and contrasting your chosen texts, as this is what the Comparative Study is all about. It is good practice to think about your texts in terms of their similarities and differences within each mode.

This approach is designed to prevent 'drift' between modes and focuses on analysis and personal response, rather than summary.

KNOW THE TEXT

# Theme/Issue - Know the Text

**1** What are your first impressions of how well characters in the tenement get along?

**2** How well is Nora treated by her neighbours in the tenement?

**3** Does Nora care about and understand her husband, Jack? Give examples to support your view.

**4** Does Jack care about and understand his wife, Nora? Give examples to support your view.

**5** What **strengths** do you see in Nora and Jack's marriage?

**6** What **weaknesses** or problems do you see in Nora and Jack's marriage?

**7** Is this a positive or negative relationship? Use examples to justify your view.

**8** Do you think Nora and Jack are a good match?

# KNOW THE TEXT

**9** Is their relationship important to Nora and Jack?

**10** Does Nora manipulate her husband?

**11** What motivated Nora to intercept Jack's letter? Do you consider this deception a betrayal?

**12** What does their argument over the letter reveal about their relationship?

## KNOW THE TEXT

**13** "I don't care if you never come back!"
Is Nora cruel to her husband when they argue?
Does he deserve her ill treatment?

**14** Does Nora's attitude to Jack change once he leaves?
Why does she search so desperately for him?

> **15** Jack chooses the Irish Citizen Army over Nora. What does this tell you about their relationship?

> **16** Nora and Jack are delighted to see one another when they are reunited in Act Three. What does their reaction suggest about their relationship?

KNOW THE TEXT

**17** Do Nora and Jack really love each other?

**18** Describe Peter and the Covey's relationship.

# THE PLOUGH AND THE STARS - THEME/ISSUE - RELATIONSHIPS

**19** What causes problems in this relationship?

**20** Is this a positive or negative relationship?

# KNOW THE TEXT

**21** Describe Bessie and Mrs Gogan's relationship.

**22** What causes problems in this relationship?

## 23 Is this a positive or negative relationship?

## 24 How do Bessie and Mrs Gogan overcome their differences and improve their relationship?

## Theme/Issue - Know the Mode

**25** Are relationships in this text generally **positive** (warm, supportive, nurturing, genuine) or **negative** (cold, cruel, destructive, false)?

**26** What makes relationships in this text complicated and **difficult**?

## 27 What would **improve** relationships in this text?

KNOW THE MODE

**28** How do relationships **change** during the story?

**29** What did **you learn** about relationships from studying this play?

**30** Are relationships **portrayed realistically** in this text? Make use of examples to support the points you make.

KNOW THE MODE

**31** Are relationships in this story **interesting** and **involving**?

**32** Did anything about the theme of relationships in this text **shock, upset** or **unsettle** you?

KNOW THE MODE

**33** What is the **most signficant relationship** in this text?
What makes it so significant and important?

**34** Do relationships in this story bring characters **happiness** or **sorrow**?

KNOW THE MODE

**35** Choose **key moments** from this story that highlight relationships in the text.

## Theme/Issue - Compare the Texts

**36** Were relationships in *The Plough and the Stars* more positive and supportive than the relationships in your other texts? Give specific examples.

**37** Rank the relationships you have studied in your various texts from most positive to most negative. Add a note to explain your choices.

**38** Were relationships in *The Plough and the Stars* the most engaging and interesting that you have studied? Explain your choice.

**39** Rank the relationships you have studied in your various texts from most interesting to least interesting. Add a note to explain your choices.

**40** Did you **learn most** about the theme of relationships from this text or another text on your comparative course?

**41** What **similarities** do you notice in the theme of relationships in this text and your other comparative texts?

COMPARE THE TEXTS

**42** What **differences** do you notice in the theme of relationships in this text and your other comparative texts?

COMPARE THE TEXTS

# Literary Genre - Know the Text

**43** How is this story told? (Consider the play format).

**44** Why is the story told in this way?
What is the effect of this?

# KNOW THE TEXT

**45** How does O'Casey create a sense of his characters in the first Act?

**46** What are your first impressions of Nora? How is her character developed?

**47**
How are the Volunteers portrayed?
Why are they portrayed this way?
How does this add to the story?

**48**
How are the British soldiers portrayed?
Why are they portrayed this way?
How does this add to the story?

# KNOW THE TEXT

**49** Comment on the setting of each Act.
What does each setting add to the story?

**50** What is the effect of the bickering of Mrs Gogan and Bessie and the Covey and Peter on the story?

**51** How does Mollser's character add to the story?

**52** Where do we see humour in the play?
What is the effect of this?

# KNOW THE TEXT

**53** How are the tenement dwellers portrayed?
Why are they portrayed like this?

**54** Comment on the imagery of the war speeches in Act Two and the language the Volunteers use. What does this add to the story?

# THE PLOUGH AND THE STARS - LITERARY GENRE

**55** Is this a play about the 1916 Rising, Dublin tenements, shared humanity or something else?

**56** What does Jack and Nora's relationship add to the story?

## KNOW THE TEXT

**57** How does the **1916 Rising** contribute to the storytelling here?

**58** Many of the play's characters are flawed.
What are their flaws?
Why has O'Casey written them this way?

**59** When this play was first performed, spectators were outraged at O'Casey's depiction of the Rising. Why were they outraged, in your opinion? Why did O'Casey choose to depict it this way?

# Literary Genre - Know the Mode

**60** Did **you** enjoy the **storyline** of the text?
Was it exciting/compelling/tense/emotional?
Why/why not?

**61** Is there just one **plot** or many plots?
What connections can you make between the storylines?

## 62. What three things interested **you** most in the story?

KNOW THE MODE

**63** Are **characters** vivid, realistic and well-developed?

**64** Do **you** empathise or **identify** with any character(s)?
*Did you become involved in this story or care about the characters? Use examples.*

**65** Who was your **favourite character**?
What aspects of this character did you enjoy?

**66** Consider Nora as the play's **heroine**. What made Nora a **memorable** or **interesting** character?

**67** Who was your **least favourite character**? What aspects of this character did you dislike? What made them a memorable or interesting character?

KNOW THE MODE

**68** Is the story humorous or tragic, romantic or realistic? Explain using examples.

**69** To what **genre** does it belong?
What aspects of this genre did you enjoy?
*Is it Romance, Thriller, Horror, Action/Adventure, Historical, Fantasy, Science-fiction, Satire, etc.?*

**70** How does the playwright create **suspense**, **high emotion** and **excitement** in the text? What **techniques** does he use to good advantage?

**71** Consider the playwright's use of **tension** and **resolution** in the play. What are the major **tensions/problems/conflicts** in the text? Are they **resolved** or not?

**72** Did the playwright make use of any striking patterns of **imagery** or **symbols** to add to the story?

**73** How does the playwright make use of the **unexpected** in this text? What did this add to the story? (Think about key moments here.)

KNOW THE MODE

**74** What is the **climax** (high point) of the story?

**75** What did **you** think of this moment?
How did it make **you feel**?

**76** Comment on the **language** of the play.
How does this spoken dimension add to the story?

**77** Comment on the **pacing** of the play.
How does this contribute to the storytelling?

**78** Comment on the **setting** of the play.
*Consider time, place, and specific locations such as the public house and the tenement. How does setting add to your understanding of the characters and their story?*

**79** Was anything about this play **moving** or **emotional**?
*Think of moments in the play that you responded to. What made them moving? How did this add to the story?*

**80** On a scale of one to ten, how much did you enjoy the **ending**? What was satisfying/unsatisfying about it? Was anything left unanswered?

**81** The experiences of seeing a play, reading a novel and viewing a film are very different.
What aspects of the **play form** worked well in this story, in your opinion?

KNOW THE MODE

**82** What did **you** like about **the way** the story was told?
*Mention aspects of storytelling and literary techniques that **you** found enjoyable. Refer to key moments.*

**83** Identify **key moments** in the play that illustrate Literary Genre (the way the story is told). Clearly **define literary techniques/ aspects of narrative** in your analysis.

KNOW THE MODE

# Literary Genre - Compare the Texts

**84** Did **you** like the way this story was told more than your other comparative texts?
*State what you enjoyed most about each.*

## COMPARE THE TEXTS

**85** Is *The Plough and the Stars* more **exciting** than your other texts?
*Consider tension, suspense, conflict, pacing and the unexpected in each of your texts.*

**86** Are **characters** more engaging in this play than in your other texts?
Refer to each of your texts in your answer.

**87** Is the **setting** more effective in telling this story than in your other texts?
Refer to each of your texts in your answer.

**88** Is this story more **unpredictable** than your other texts?
Refer to each of your texts in your answer.

COMPARE THE TEXTS

**89** Did this play have greater **emotional power** than your other texts?
Was this emotional power created in a more interesting way here or in a different text?

**90** What **similarities** do you notice in the Literary Genre of this play and your other comparative texts?
*Mention specific aspects of narrative.*

COMPARE THE TEXTS

**91** What **differences** do you notice in the Literary Genre of this play and your other comparative texts?
*Mention specific aspects of narrative.*

COMPARE THE TEXTS

# General Vision and Viewpoint - Know the Text

**92** Mrs Gogan's remarks as the play opens point to the bad in characters. How does this affect the atmosphere and feel of this opening section?

**93** Do the characters get along together as the play begins? What sense do you get of what life is like for them from this?

# KNOW THE TEXT

**94** "I do be terrible afraid I'll die sometime when I'm be meself..." How does Mollser's arrival at the end of Act One affect the mood?

**95** "Bloodshed is a cleansing and sanctifying thing..." How is dying for Ireland described in Act Two?

# THE PLOUGH AND THE STARS - GENERAL VISION AND VIEWPOINT

**96** "...it's a derogatory thing..."

Do disagreements and rows colour every aspect of these characters' lives?

**97** "Death for th' Independence of Ireland!"
Do you get the sense that this is a worthy cause? Do the ordinary citizens appreciate this sacrifice and struggle?

# KNOW THE TEXT

**98** How does the outbreak of fighting in Dublin's streets add to the atmosphere?

**99** "My Jack will be killed...butchered as a sacrifice to th' dead!"
What view is O'Casey expressing here?

**100** In Act Three, none of the men assist the woman making her way towards Rathmines. What outlook is suggested by their actions?

**101** Mrs Gogan and Bessie are at odds for much of the play, but go looting together. Do you see their alliance as a positive or negative development?

# KNOW THE TEXT

**102** Do characters put their differences aside and pull together once fighting breaks out?
What does this tell us about people and life?

**103** How does the closing section make you feel?
*Use 'I' statements to develop your Personal Response.*

# THE PLOUGH AND THE STARS - GENERAL VISION AND VIEWPOINT

**104** How does the **ending** reflect O'Casey's view of life?

**105** Is there any hope for the tenement dwellers as the play ends, or is their future bleak?

## KNOW THE TEXT

**106** What do the deaths of Mollser, Nora's baby, Jack and Bessie contribute to the General Vision and Viewpoint of the play?

**107** What is Seán O'Casey telling us about life in this story?
*What is Seán O'Casey's message?*
*Is his outlook positive or negative, in your view?*

## General Vision and Viewpoint - Know the Mode

**108** Identify bright/hopeful/optimistic aspects of the play.

**109** Identify dark/hopeless/pessimistic aspects of the play.

| 110 | Is this text **optimistic** or **pessimistic**? Explain. *Consider characters' safety and future outlook.* |

| 111 | On a scale of one to ten, how optimistic is this text? |

**112** Identify the **aspects of life** that the playwright concentrates on.
Are they positive or negative?
*Consider rebellion, naivity, bravery, determination, struggle, compassion, etc.*

## 113 What **comments** do characters make on their **society** and the problems they're facing?

**114** Are characters happy or unhappy?

# THE PLOUGH AND THE STARS - GENERAL VISION AND VIEWPOINT

**115** What makes characters in this story happy and fulfilled?
What does this tell us about their view of life?

**116** What makes characters in this story unhappy and unfulfilled?
What does this tell us about their view of life?

**117** Are **relationships** destructive or nurturing? What do they reveal about life, as we see characters supported/thwarted in their efforts to grow/mature?

KNOW THE MODE

**118** Are **imagery** and **language** bright or dark in the text? (Tone of the text)

89

# THE PLOUGH AND THE STARS – GENERAL VISION AND VIEWPOINT

**119** What is the **mood** of this text?

**120** What does this story **teach us about life?**
*What do we learn about life's hardships? Are struggles overcome? Is determination rewarded? Is life difficult or joyful?*

**121** How do you **feel** as you watch this play?
*Refer to key moments to anchor your answer.*

# 122 How do you **feel** at the **end**?

**123** Are **questions** raised by the text **resolved** by the end?
Are they resolved **happily** or **unhappily**?

**124** Are **you hopeful** or **despairing** regarding the prospects for human **happiness** in this story?
*Are characters likely to be happy?*

**125** Identify the **key moments** in the play that illustrate the General Vision and Viewpoint of the text.

KNOW THE MODE

## General Vision and Viewpoint - Compare the Texts

**126** Is life happier for characters in this story than in your other comparative texts? Explain.

## COMPARE THE TEXTS

**127** Do characters in this text face more obstacles and difficulties than in your other texts?
Who struggles most?

**128** Are characters in this text **rewarded more** for their struggles than in your other texts?
By overcoming adversity, do they achieve true happiness and contentment in a way that is not realised in your other texts?

**129** Is this the brightest, most hopeful and triumphant text you have studied? Explain why its message is more or less positive than your other texts.

**130** Which of your chosen texts was the bleakest and most upsetting or depressing?
*Explain why it was more negative than your other texts. What made them more positive?*

COMPARE THE TEXTS

**131** Plot your three texts on a scale of one to ten, from darkest (most pessimistic) to brightest (most optimistic). Add points to explain their position.

**132** What **similarities** do you notice in the General Vision and Viewpoint of this text and your other comparative texts?

COMPARE THE TEXTS

**133** What **differences** do you notice in the General Vision and Viewpoint of this text and your other comparative texts?

COMPARE THE TEXTS

www.ingramcontent.com/pod-product-compliance
Lightning Source LLC
Chambersburg PA
CBHW050714090526
44587CB00019B/3369